Maui

An Introduction

A stunning combination of lush mountains, stark volcanic craters, gold to white sand beaches, and luminous tropic seas provide Maui with an ever-present natural beauty. But more than the obvious attractions make Maui what it is, for its beauty is matched by the heartfelt aloha of its people, a long and varied history, and an imaginative range of attractions and activities designed to take advantage of all that Maui has to offer. Throw in a steady supply of clear skies and ample doses of sunshine, and it's easy to understand the saying *"Maui no ka oi,"* Maui is the best.

Lahaina & Kaanapali

Lahaina was once the whaling capital of the world. Many of its historic landmarks have been preserved, giving the visitor a firsthand experience into Maui's past.

Snorkelers float in Maui's lustrous seas off Kaanapali, Maui's most famous destination resort.

While there's no pressure to do anything more strenuous than relax on the beach, Maui's vibrantly clear waters are an irresistible temptation.

Maui offers Hawaii's greatest concentration of tennis courts.

The Pacific Ocean frames many of Maui's exquisitely situated and beautifully maintained golf courses.

Whale Watching

The tail of a giant humpback rises high above the water's surface as it prepares to dive. In the background, West Maui canefields.

Canefields cover West Maui lowlands that lie between Lahaina and the West-Maui Mountains.

Canefields sprawl over the Maui landscape.

Inset: Flowering cane.

A pineapple ready for harvest.

Iao Needle

Iao Needle, a Maui landmark, rises 1,200 feet from the heart of the deeply eroded West Maui Mountains.

The exotic protea has become a popular flower exported from Maui.

Seven Sacred Pools

◄ **The Seven Pools were formed by the erosive power of a stream that cut its way through accumulated soil into the underlying lava rock.**

▲ **Fields of taro cover the Keanae Peninsula, halfway to Hana.**

Haleakala

Sunrise atop Haleakala crater is a breathtaking experience.

Haleakala Crater was created from a volcano that last erupted about 1790. The crater is 7 1/2 miles long, 2 1/2 miles wide, and 3,000 feet deep.

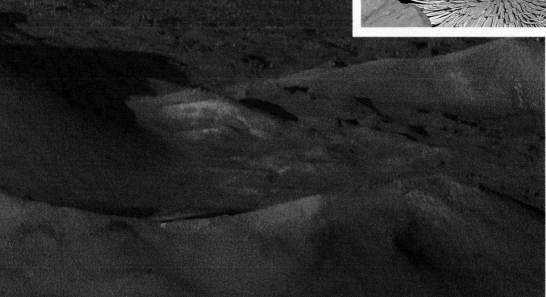

A blossoming Silversword, one of Haleakala's unique natives.

Beaches

◄ **An aerial view of Kaanapali's magnificent shoreline.**
▲ **Visitors and residents create a colorful mosaic on Kamaole Beach, Kihei coast of Maui.**

Sunbathing on Wailea's Mokapu Beach. In the distance, Kahoolawe sits on the western horizon. The crater-rim island of Molokini, popular with divers and snorkelers for its coral and tropical fish, lies between Maui and Kahoolawe.

Pineapple fields surround West Maui beaches at Makuleia, Fleming Park, and Oneloa. In the distance, villas of the elegant Kapalua Resort.

The red sands of Kaihalulu
Beach in Hana were formed
from the rock of the
surrounding cinder cone.

Puu Olai, a small coastal cinder cone, forms the northern boundary of Makena Beach.

Hana

Hana is nestled between a large bay from which it takes its name, and the verdant hillsides of the Hana Ranch.

◄ Torch ginger is one of the many tropical flowers that grow abundantly in Hana.

The warmth of Hana expressed through a friendly smile.

▼ On the east side of Maui is Hana. Waterfalls tucked in steep cliffs are in abundance.

Luscious papaya and avocado grow profusely in Hana.

After West Maui's volcanic
fires had died, wind and
rain carved jagged contours
into its original uncreased
dome. Then nature softened
these valleys with lush
greenery.

Pailolo Channel

Honokohau
Bay
Lipoa Point   Nakal
Honokohau
Fleming Beach   Honokohua
Napili Bay   Kahaku
Kahana
Camp   Mahinahina Camp
Honokowai   1423
Camp
Kahana Strm.
Honokowai Strm.
Kaanapali   Puukolii
Kekaa Pt.
4480. E
Kepani
The Nee
Hanakaoo
Point   Crater   Puu Kukui 5788   22
Mala   Lahainaluna
Kahoma   School
Petroglyphs   (First Printing Press)
Lahaina   Wainee
Iao Valley State
Launiupoko

Auau Channel
Launiupoko Pt.
Kaiwaloa
Olowalu Pet
Olowalu   HONOAPIIL
Hekili Point   Mopua

Papa

Kukui Point

1443
KAHOOLAW
1161
531

Kealaikahiki
Point
Kamohio Bay
Kuakaiwa Pt.

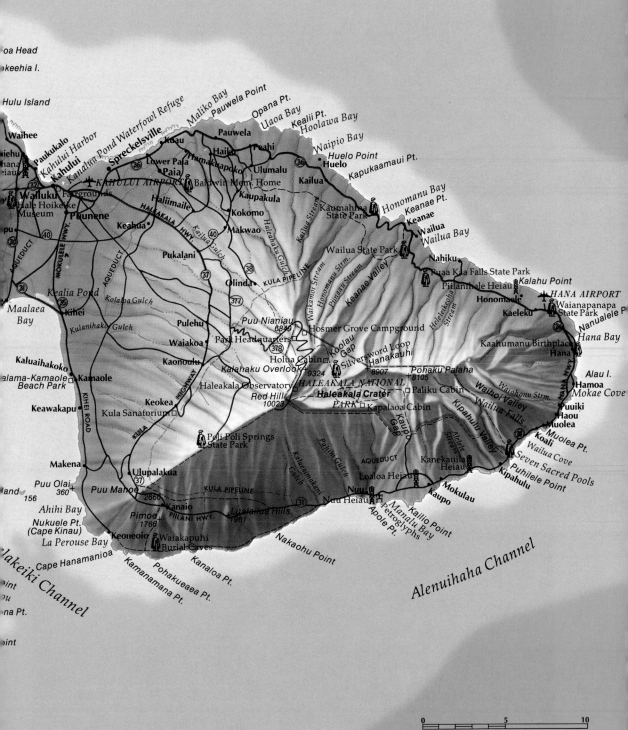

oa Head

keehia I.

Hulu Island

Waihee

iehu

iau
Kahului Harbor   Maliko Bay   Pauwela Point
Paukakalo   Kanalua Pond Waterfowl Refuge   Opana Pt.

Wailuku   Kahului   Spreckelsville   Kuau   Haiku   Uaoa Bay   Kealii Pt.

Hale Hoikeke   Fairgrounds   Lower Paia   Hamakuapoko   Peahi   Hoolawa Bay

Museum   KAHULUI AIRPORT   Paia   Pauwela   Waipio Bay

Puunene   Baldwin Mem. Home   Ulumalu   Huelo Point

pu   Keahua   Haliimaile   Kaupakula   Kailua   Huelo   Kapukaamaui Pt.

Kokomo   Honomanu Bay

Makawao   Kaumahina   Keanae Pt.
State Park   Keanae

Pukalani   Wailua
Wailua Bay

Olinda   Wailua State Park   Nahiku

Kealia Pond   KULA PIPELINE   Puaa Kaa Falls State Park

Kolaipa Gulch   Piilanihale Heiau   Kalahu Point

Maalaea
Bay   Kihei   Pulehu   Puu Nianiau   Honomaele   HANA AIRPORT

Kulanihakoi Gulch   6849   Hosmer Grove Campground   Kaeleku   Waianapanapa State Park

Waiakoa   Park Headquarters   Koolau   Hana Bay

Kaluaihakoko   Holua Cabin   Gap   Silversword Loop   Kaahumanu Birthplace

lama-Kamaole   Kamaole   Kaonoulu   Kalahaku Overlook   Hanakauhi   Hana

Beach Park   Haleakala Observatory   9324   Pohaku Palaha   Alau I.

Keawakapu   Keokea   Red Hill   HALEAKALA NATIONAL   8907   8105   Hamoa

10023   Haleakala Crater   Paliku Cabin   Mokae Cove

Kula Sanatorium   PARK   Kapalaoa Cabin   Puuiki

Poli Poli Springs   Haou

Makena   State Park   Muolea

Puu Olai   Ulupalakua   Koali

360   Puu Mahoe   Kanekauila   Wailua Cove

156   KULA PIPELINE   Heiau   Seven Sacred Pools

Ahihi Bay   Kanaio   Puhilele Point

Nukuele Pt.   Pimoe   Lualailua Hills   Loaloa Heiau   Kipahulu

(Cape Kinau)   1766   1961   Nuu   Mokulau

La Perouse Bay   PIILANI HWY.   Nuu Heiau   Kaupo

Keoneoio   Waiakapuhi   Petroglyphs

Burial Caves   Kailio Point

Cape Hanamanioa   Pohakueaea Pt.   Kanaloa Pt.   Nakaohu Point   Apole Pt.

Kamanamana Pt.

lakeiki Channel

int

ou

na Pt.

int

Alenuihaha Channel

0   5   10

STATUTE MILES

A diver tosses a lei into the surf from Kaanapali's Black Rock.